W9-BZG-193

Withdrawn
Horsham Township Library

Horsham Township Library
435 Babylon Road
Horsham, PA 19044-1224
215-443-2609
www.HorshamLibrary.org

Pebble® Plus

Marine Mammals

California Sea Lions

by Megan Cooley Peterson

Consulting editor: Gail Saunders-Smith, PhD

Consultant: Kathryn A. Ono, PhD
Associate Professor, Department of Marine Sciences
University of New England, Biddeford, Maine

CAPSTONE PRESS
a capstone imprint

Pebble Plus is published by Capstone Publishers,
1710 Roe Crest Drive, North Mankato, MN 56003
www.capstonepub.com

Copyright © 2013 by Capstone Press, a Capstone imprint. All rights reserved.
No part of this publication may be reproduced in whole or in part, or stored in a retrieval system, or transmitted in any
form or by any means, electronic, mechanical, photocopying, recording, or otherwise, without written permission of the
publisher. For information regarding permission, write to Capstone Press,
1710 Roe Crest Drive, North Mankato, MN 56003.

Library of Congress Cataloging-in-Publication Data
Peterson, Megan Cooley.
California sea lions / by Megan Cooley Peterson.
p. cm.—(Pebble plus. Marine mammals)
Includes bibliographical references and index.
Summary: "Simple text and full-color photographs provide a brief introduction to California sea lions"—Provided
by publisher.
ISBN 978-1-4296-8573-3 (library binding)
ISBN 978-1-62065-311-1 (Ebook PDF)
1. California sea lion—Juvenile literature. I. Title.
QL737.P63P396 2013
599.79'75—dc23   2011052369

Editorial Credits
Jeni Wittrock, editor; Ted Williams, designer; Svetlana Zhurkin, media researcher; Kathy McColley,
production specialist

Photo Credits
Alamy: E.R. Degginger, 21, Jeff Mondragon, 9; Dreamstime: Lianquan Yu (seal), 8; iStockphoto: David Gomez, cover;
Minden Pictures: Flip Nicklin, 15; National Geographic Stock: James A. Sugar, 7; Newscom: Photoshot/Evolve/Franco
Banfi, 11; SeaPics: Mark Jones, 17; Shutterstock: lfstewart, 13, mcherevan (splash), cover, 1, Mikhail Dudarev (water
texture), cover, 1, Nagel Photography, 5, Sebastien Burel, 19, visceralimage, 3

Note to Parents and Teachers

The Marine Mammals series supports national science standards related to life science.
This book describes and illustrates California sea lions. The images support early readers in
understanding the text. The repetition of words and phrases helps early readers learn new
words. This book also introduces early readers to subject-specific vocabulary words, which are
defined in the Glossary section. Early readers may need assistance to read some words and to
use the Table of Contents, Glossary, Read More, Internet Sites, and Index sections of the book.

Printed in the United States of America in North Mankato, Minnesota.
042012   006682CGF12

Table of Contents

Chatty Sea Lions

Bark! Bark!

California sea lions are

chatty marine mammals.

They talk to each other

with barks and grunts.

California sea lions live
in the Pacific Ocean.
They rest along the coasts
of Mexico, the United States,
and Canada.

California Sea Lion Range

■ where California sea lions swim

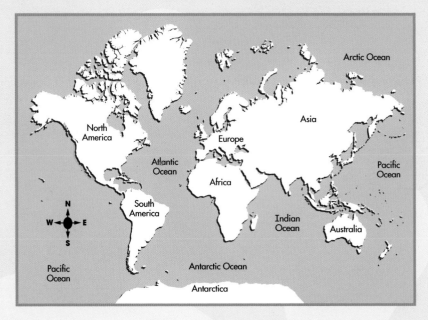

A California Sea Lion's Body

Splash! California sea lions swim with flippers that look like paddles. They walk on land by turning their back flippers forward.

 **California sea lion:** 8 feet (2.4 meters) long

 5 feet (1.5 m) long

California sea lions' bodies
are suited for life underwater.
These animals see and hear well.
Flaps cover their ears. They feel
for food with their whiskers.

Brrr! Life in the ocean

can be cold.

Hair and blubber keep

California sea lions warm.

They shed their hair once a year.

13

California sea lions stay at sea

for days or weeks. They can

dive deeper than 600 feet

(183 meters). A sea lion

holds its breath while diving.

California sea lions are smart and playful animals. Young sea lions learn to swim all by themselves. They surf the rolling ocean waves.

California Sea Lion Life Cycle

California sea lions come to shore in May and June. Females then give birth to a single pup. Hundreds of sea lions might gather in one area.

Mothers and pups know each other's call and smell. They can always find each other. After one year, the pups live alone. California sea lions live 20 years or more.

Glossary

blubber—a thick layer of fat under the skin of some animals; blubber keeps animals warm

coast—land next to an ocean or sea

flipper—one of the broad, flat limbs of a sea creature

mammal—a warm-blooded animal that breathes air; mammals have hair or fur; female mammals feed milk to their young

marine—living in salt water

pup—a young California sea lion

shore—the place where the ocean meets land

whisker—a long stiff hair growing on the face and bodies of some animals

Read More

Coleman, Miriam. *Swimming with Sea Lions.* Flippers and Fins. New York: PowerKids Press, 2010.

Gallagher, Debbie. *Seals and Sea Lions.* Zoo Animals. New York: Marshall Cavendish Benchmark, 2010.

Metz, Lorijo. *Discovering Sea Lions.* Along the Shore. New York: PowerKids Press, 2012.

Internet Sites

FactHound offers a safe, fun way to find Internet sites related to this book. All of the sites on FactHound have been researched by our staff.

Here's all you do:

Visit *www.facthound.com*

Type in this code: 9781429685733

Super-cool stuff! Check out projects, games and lots more at **www.capstonekids.com**

23

Index

Word Count: 215
Grade: 1
Early-Intervention Level: 16

Horsham Township Library